The Seven Gates:

A Memoir of a Descent

by

Elaine Amyot

Attic Owl Books
Dieppe, New Brunswick

© 2010 Elaine Amyot

Cover artwork © Elaine Amyot
Femme et serpent

Author Photo by Gilles LeBlanc

All illustrations are by the author,
Except *Portrait of Elaine* by Yvon Gallant

All rights reserved. No part of this publication can be reproduced, stored in a retrieval system, or transmitted in any form or by any means, electronic, mechanical, photocopying, or recording, without prior permission of the publisher and/or author, except by a reviewer who may quote brief passages in a review.

Amyot, Elaine

The Seven Gates: A Memoir of a Descent

ISBN: 978-0-9780510-4-4

First paperback edition 2010

Attic Owl Books
379 Beausejour Street
Dieppe, NB E1A 1Y5

E-mail : eepond@rogers.com

Printed in the United States of America
By www.lulu.com

For Ed

Tell all the Truth but tell it slant –
Success in Circuit lies
Too bright for our infirm Delight
The Truth's superb surprise

As Lightning to the Children eased
With explanation kind
The Truth must dazzle gradually
Or every man be blind –

- Emily Dickinson

Prologue

In an ancient Sumerian myth, recorded on clay tablets that are approximately 5,000 years old, the Goddess Inanna abandons heaven and descends to the underworld. Why she does this is never quite clear. Before her descent she tells a trusted female servant to appeal to the gods for help if she does not return within three days. There are seven gates to the "land of no return," and at each gate one piece of her regalia is taken, so that finally, when she reaches bottom, she is stripped bare, killed and her corpse hung on a peg to rot. This is ordered by the Goddess of the Underworld, Ereshkigal, who is Inanna's sister. Ereshkigal wants Inanna brought "naked and bowed low."

The faithful servant is able to arrange for Inanna's return. Inanna returns but only after agreeing to find persons to take her place in the underworld. Her consort and his sister are ordered to each spend one half year in the underworld. They are placed in the hands of the eternal holy Ereshkigal. The poem ends with the words, "Ereshkigal, sweet is your praise."

The myth of Inanna shows the way for a life-enhancing descent into the abyss of the dark Goddess and out again. Inanna descends, submits, dies, and then by willingness to receive, is lifted up again. She sheds her old identity, is reduced to primal matter and is reborn. The myth is a description of a pattern of psychological health for the feminine. It closely parallels the stages I went through in my descent and in my resurfacing.

Gate One

At the entry to Gate One
I am stripped of a piece of my regalia:
My energy and vitality

On November First, 1984, I have a dream of going up a hill. It is dark, snow is falling, the road is icy. I am on my stomach on a skateboard, trying to ascend the dangerously steep hill on the wrong side of the road.

*

I say to myself, "I can't go on."

*

When I wake up, I telephone the principal of the school where I teach and tell him exactly that.

*

I take a leave of absence from teaching, to face a severe depression and a state of exhaustion.

A friend suggests that I see Dr. H., a psychiatrist new to our area. For a year I see him regularly. He is a man of formidable presence, large with powerful looking hands, silver grey eyes, eyebrows that are bushy, wide but pointed and upturned at the ends. His gaze is penetrating – there will be few secrets from him. Merlin the wizard enchanter must have looked like him, and I have a feeling of something magical about to happen.

He encourages me to open to a memory that I had kept encapsulated for almost fifty years. It had become a dark stone that was now very heavy. This burden was the result of a small incident that I was never able to talk about – not even to my mother. At the time it was just absorbed silently. My mother told me later that I did not speak a word for two months that winter. Photographs at that time show me to be serious, no longer an innocent happy child but one seeming to hold something back, unable to trust. I did not understand that this small event was the reason for my silence, my loss of appetite, and my lack of interest in the usual games.

It was the winter of the coronation year – 1937. My best friend Georgette and I did not pay much attention to news of the forthcoming celebration, but two presents that Georgette had received made it very real. Each of these objects was of metal with very intense colours, royal blue, deep red and much gold. One was a miniature coach – a duplicate of the one to be used by the new king and his family. The coach, with horses, was so impressive that we could not play with it. Instead, we would gaze at it and imagine ourselves to be the two princesses, Elizabeth and Margaret Rose, who wore such magnificent gowns of white satin, purple trains and small crowns.

The other object that made the year 1937 significant was a brooch in the form of a crown that Rose Savignac had given to Georgette. Rose was the daughter of our landlady – Mme Savignac – a woman whom we never saw smiling. She had a closed face, lips that opened only to bark out orders. It was a surprise to us that Rose was tender, smiling and seemed to love us. She was nice to me too, but when she gave a brooch to Georgette she did not give one to me. I did not question this at the time, but accepted it as a child accepts her world not knowing any other.

But another incident happened that winter that was more troublesome, even though I accepted it too – or, more accurately, I let it happen. It was on an early winter evening. The sky was that beautiful deep blue when stars first come out and I was about to get into a snowsuit of that same blue, a snow suit that had leather patches, leather that had a texture that looked like a hen had walked over it leaving little lined indentations. It had a colourful crest on its pocket. I don't remember the design but I remember how wonderful were the silk threads on its underside. The colours were so vibrant that they seemed to move. I had never seen colours so smooth and alive.

  I was leaving Rose Savignac's house to go to supper in my place, one door away. Rose was no longer there but her big brother Maurice was. He helped me put my legs in the pants part of the one-piece snow suit, but before sliding the zipper he suddenly placed his hand in my underpants and very softly felt my genitals – a part of me that at that age was a no-name. Time slowed to a crawl, while he went on and on. I suggested in a small voice that this was something my mother did not want me to do, but this did not stop him. What was curious to me was that he never spoke to me or looked at my face.

I was not surprised to feel some pleasure, for in the past that no-name part of me had given me comfort when touched. Now, however, this familiar sensation was overlaid with a bewildering feeling of unease. I felt sad, alone, lost. I could not talk to my mother or my father, and so a void was created. This feeling of falling into a dark hole, of being a non-person, of having no worth, of losing my sense of self, of not existing – this feeling still recurs, triggered by situations where I think (sometimes erroneously) that I am not valued or even noticed.

Gate Two

At the entry to Gate Two
I am stripped of a piece of my regalia:
My inner compass

During the year of darkness (1985) I begin to work with oil pastels, using a black gouache resist. This is a technique that I enjoyed teaching in the classroom. I like the floating print-like effect. The colours are brilliant, thick-textured and waxy, vivid and intense. Perhaps I am hoping that the bright hues will encourage me to emerge from the ever-present depression, but that does not happen. Instead of the joyful, colourful images that I expected, there appear images that are bleak and lacking in vitality.

For instance, the tree of life, although crowned with abundant red and yellow fruit, is rooted in a snowy landscape – a night scene. This snow is not a pristine white but a dull grey due to the effects of the resist.

The Tree of Life

The same grey-white is present in the image of a woman's face, featureless except for very large, green and golden eyes that lack pupils:

Anima Guide

In the image of a grey left hand attempting to grasp succulent-looking fruit that are just barely out of reach:

L'action

And in the image of a leafless tree alone in a dull-green land with six white moons showing the passage of time:

Lunar Opus

An image appears that I do not understand at this time. It is of a doll-girl lying sprawled under a tree, her articulated limbs lifeless. She is unaware of the colourful wild flowers about her, for there is a sack covering her head.

Doll Image of the Soul

There is a recurring theme of a woman in red, rigid with fear among trees, herself becoming part tree. But what it takes me so long to see is that she is not leaving a forest, but entering one – leaving behind colourful meadows, mountains and bright sky. A short time later I realize that these works are prophetic, for I am diagnosed with having a life-threatening illness – a form of cancer called Hodgkin's disease.

L'entrée dans la forêt – Danger

Like the woman in red I am entering a dark forest, an unknown place with no visible path. I remember Dante's famous lines:

Nel mezzo del cammin di nostra vita
Mi ritrovai per una selva oscura,
Che' la diritta via era smarrita.

In the middle of the journeys of our life
I found myself in a dark wood,
For I had lost the right path.

*

I am lost and full of fear. There is a part of me that is now very heavy, a dark part that has been put in a sack since the Savignac episode. To find the right path means finding the lost part and discovering what has been hidden.

For fifty years I have lived with fear. Fear that my secret will be discovered. A secret I try to hide, using up a lot of energy in the process. The secret is that I am worthless. I must do my utmost to put across the idea that I am intelligent, competent, and talented. Love is not given freely but must be earned.

The waste of energy is phenomenal. I can no longer function. I have lost my way. There is no north, no south, no east or west. I am close to death.

Gate 3

At the entry to Gate Three
I am stripped of a piece of my regalia:
My health

One day in a shopping mall I encounter a colleague whom I have not seen in a decade. When she asks me how I am, I point to the turban I am wearing (it hides the effects of chemotherapy) and I say that I have cancer. She responds immediately with: "You must see Father Bujold. Here is his telephone number. And remember: THIS IS NOT A COINCIDENCE."

These 'non-coincidences' happen several times during the descent, and they are always unexpected, always helpful and always bring me closer to the path that will lead me out of the forest.

When I telephone Raymond Bujold for an appointment I am surprised to hear only a terse "Mardi prochain à 8 heures?" ("Next Tuesday at 8 a.m.?"). He asks none of the questions I expect a therapist to ask. I am to discover that he is a man who has no use for unnecessary words.

I set out, leaving my house with a cold feeling of apprehension and fear. What if, I ask myself. What if this priest-therapist believes that illness is a punishment from God? What if he judges me to be of little faith and tells me that to get better I need to confess my sins? I have no faith – I am lost in a forest with no way out. There is no centre, no beginning.

The feeling of dread begins to ebb as I follow the river toward Raymond's retreat at 'La Solitude.' This tidal river, flowing to the sea and returning to its source, is a connection with life that helps replace my fear with some calm. It is even more comforting to turn from the main road to a small woods with a view of the river and some paths, one of which leads to a log house, Raymond's La Solitude. The log house is honey-coloured, with tall trees close to it, seeming to protect it. A rabbit sits unafraid under a tree proving that this is indeed a sanctuary. I breathe in the spicy clean smell of pine and spruce, and I feel that I've come to a safe place, a home.

Once inside La Solitude I am struck by the view from a tall window, conscious of nothing else but the sight of birch and spruce trees so close to this window that they seem about to enter the room.

*

Trees have always been important to me, and in my childhood they were more important than people. On 92 St. Thomas Street, Joliette, where I lived as a small child during the Depression, there were no lawns, no flower beds, only that invasive Bishop's weed, and in front of our house, one small lone maple tree. I befriended this tree by touching it gently and it returned my affections by giving me sap in the spring from a small opening which was at just the right height for me to lick its sweet water. This tree was a friend, one that did not taunt me for being 'une maudite protestante.' I didn't know what this meant but I knew that it was something I *was*, something that I couldn't do anything about, something shameful that set me apart from others.

In the back yard on St. Thomas Street Mother and I planted an acorn and watched it grow to become a tiny seedling – expecting it to become a tall oak some day, like the ones in Tante Lily's woods. (It was not to be, for M. Dugas, our new landlord, trampled it while mending a nearby fence.) In Tante Lily's woods were some young pine trees, only a little taller than I, with soft fragrant needles that were gentle to the touch and that accepted me, unlike my aggressive cousins who spent their summers at their Grandmother's – my (great) Tante Lily. These cousins were everything I felt I was not – they were big, healthy, well-dressed, sure of themselves, unafraid to express themselves, and had the magic English name of Stonehouse. I annoyed them because in their colouring books (my father forbade us these; he wanted us to make our own drawings, our own lines, and not meekly accept another's version of reality) I used only one colour – a beautiful delicate mauve – and refused to colour within the black lines. The colour was too beautiful to be restricted.

    One day in these woods I wandered away from the cousins and found myself in a small clearing, surrounded by birch trees. There I had an experience I've seldom talked about because it is impossible to describe well. There was a feeling of being complete, a feeling of light, of beauty. There were no boundaries, no limitations, no sense of time. This happened only the once but I have never lost hope that it will happen again.

*

In Raymond's presence I know I have come to sanctuary. If I were to die, he would help me with that process. If I choose to live, he will help me with that more difficult task.

The therapy sessions with Raymond last one hour during which I enter a dream-like world, a vivid place, inhabited by strange creatures or vaguely familiar persons. To access this underworld I need to let go of my 'grand cerveau' (my ego) – the part of me that is in control, that is conscious. This 'letting go' is difficult, for I have to do it in spite of a fear similar to the one experienced before jumping in water from a great height. There is also a greater fear, the fear that once I 'let go' I will not find my way back. Raymond assures me that this will not happen, that he will be my guide.

I would lie down on a mat on the floor next to Raymond's chair, near the window framing the friendly trees. It is comforting to sense the presence of these trees and to know that nearby is the tidal river that I love. Raymond places a soft woolen blanket over me, then asks me to take deep breaths and relax. I am to tell him which part of my body is ill-at-ease, wanting to be noticed. This is the access point. During our first session it is my right eye. Its lid will not stop quivering. Raymond asks if I could look into that eye. When I do I am looking into a blazing, seething, red volcano. It will not erupt then, but after being assured that the lava-rage flowing out will not leave me empty of life, I am able to let the heavy lava flow.

Woman Letting Go of Rage

The work with Raymond seems to take an eternity. Then he does what he always does at the end of one of these episodes: he guides me to a place that is serene, beautiful. It is a sheltered cove where I can let the sun's rays touch my naked body and then I can immerse myself in the warm seawater.

I leave La Solitude sometimes feeling disoriented, but always free of anxiety and heaviness.

Once home I transfer the images to coloured paper, using scissors to cut out the forms. The chemotherapy has affected my vision and makes my hands tremble so that drawing or using a paint brush is not possible.

This sculpting in colour is a technique I still use today.

The sessions trigger memories from my past, and I begin to write them down.

In the other kingdom everything around me seems changed and I know I am different. I have no hair, my eyesight is dim, my face swollen and yellowish, my hands tremble. I can no longer draw but I do not give up my expressing what I am experiencing. What I can't do with paints or pencils I discover I can do with coloured paper and scissors.

This sculpting in paper, a friend tells me, is what Matisse did in his bed-ridden years. Later, when I see some of his works of that period, I realize the similarity.

At first the plant forms, unlike his, are pale without fruit or flower.

Plants, Without Fruit or Flower

Snakes are often in my work at this time. They are a symbol of life renewing itself and therefore a sign of hope.

La peur sur le champ de bataille

One work done at this time, after walking in a real forest, is of three trees on a black paper. The trees have no foliage but are interlaced. The ground is strewn with sack-like objects, some white, others black. None of the black ones are open.

Vie interieure: pré d'en haut

A nun friend interprets this work as one showing that my illness (a grey time) is being held up by a strong red tree and a young green one. She tells me I am strong and will leave the dark forest. The sacks will be opened gradually. But while still there, in the other kingdom, I can never sleep well, so I listen to late night music and record the names of musicians and compositions in a small red book.

In this book I also write down dreams, and names of the many medications I agree to take. Some frighten. Before injecting me with a certain one the doctor tells me that for a very few it is fatal. Will I be among the very few? I learn to look at fear and decide to go on in spite of it. I cannot pray but a priest tells me that this illness is a form of prayer that others pray for me.

I give up health. I am uncoordinated, ill, 'out of touch' with myself.

Gate 4

At the entry to Gate Four
I am stripped of a piece of my regalia:
My sense of autonomy, of being in charge of my life

In further therapy sessions with Raymond he asks me to visualize a safe place, a place that can be accessed whenever I need to find a refuge from the ominous gloom of the dark kingdom. This is a difficult task and not a very successful one, for the safe place that appears is a small red house on the other side of a wide river – far away.

Beside it is a stone bench, unprotected but with a soft blanket thrown over it – a blanket whose texture and colour changes each time I visualize it.

Sometimes it is a soft rose silk, other times a warm earth-coloured wool, or a blue-green harlequin-patterned heavy satin. It is comforting to be covered by these and makes the hardness of the stone bearable.

Mon guide s'en va

A more beneficial find is that of a small, imagined disc that I can hold in the palm of my hand over my solar plexus. This is a sun disc, of a bright gold, and like the sun it gives out a warmth that permeates every cell of my body.

Raymond often asks me during the imagery to walk along an imagined beach. He tells me that I will discover a helpful animal. I enjoy the feel of warm sand under my bare feet, the sight and sound of the ocean, the feel of the sun on my body. It is a surprise to find a small hermit crab – not a large strong animal that I thought would be helpful such as a horse or a lion.

I identify with the small creature that needs a shell, a protective dwelling, and of course the astrological sign is cancer. I become humbled and realize that I need to accept help.

Woman Full of Love,
With Hermit Crab, Etc.

At the same time of discovering Bernard l'hermit (French for a hermit crab), I find a beautiful white shell, one that holds silence, something I need to listen to. To heal I need to be still, to be silent. To do this I learn to meditate – something I find very difficult at first, for my thoughts hurtle through my mind at a violent rate. Eventually I am able to let go of the fear of the hooded figure, hand upraised in warning, that prevents me from allowing the warm dark silence to be reached. It is a welcoming darkness, full of love. It is home.

Solitude l'amour entre

Several weeks into therapy, after the finding of a safe place – including a sun disc, a hermit crab, and a shell – comes the most important discovery. As I walk along the now familiar beach I become conscious of a presence beside me – on my left. I never see the face of this presence but I do see that it is clothed in white, a shining white that radiates light. I feel that it is Christ. As we walk together, with my left hand held by his right hand, I am enveloped by a sense of peace, of oneness, of timelessness. Later I will realize that this experience is central to my healing.

I have lost my sense of autonomy but with the guidance of the therapist I have discovered a special animal and a Christ figure. I have gained strength with these discoveries. Like Innana at the 4th gate, however, I do not realize that there are to be other stages in the descent; that the bottom has not yet been reached.

Gate 5

At the entry to Gate Five
I am stripped of a piece of my regalia:
My voice

With Raymond as guide I am also able to go deeper into dreams and into childhood memories. I am able to re-experience past events, to do collages of them, and to let them go.

In one of the sessions I am at my mother's knee. I am very young, perhaps three. We live on Tâché Street, before my brother's birth. We are at a neighbour's – Mrs. Hogg. It is a Ladies' aide meeting. We have delicious thin salmon and celery sandwiches. The crusts have been cut off. My mother sits there, not speaking. I can feel her fear. I do not know how to help her. I remain still. I eat the sandwich. I look at the curtain of small brass beads that covers the doorway to the kitchen.

Once home, after this session with Raymond, the collage I do is with torn paper except for the figure of the mother. I cut her out of brown paper. She has a crown of thorns, an X over her bosom, hiding her green, red heart.

A cord leads from her to me, a small child. Over my heart is a black sack – not mine, tied to the brown link of a cord to the mother.

Mother Fear Child

When I was ten my mother could not understand why I had such difficulty in getting to sleep. I couldn't tell her about the man. To talk about him would be to admit that he frightened me and I wanted him out of my dream world. He came silently. I never saw his face, for before I could turn around and open my eyes he had slipped a sack over my head. It was a pillowcase, which he tied around my throat with a rope. Holding this he would lead me off the bed, into the living room, out of the house and throughout our town. In the morning I would wake up tired but relieved to be able to breathe freely once more.

*

The year was 1942. These were dark times.
THE WAR.

*

Charles, my favourite uncle, had been living with us, but with the war he had joined the RCAF and was reported 'missing in action.' Every evening we listened to war news. Charles was a rear gunner in a Lancaster – we knew that this was very dangerous but not knowing where he was flying made us even more anxious. We would not talk about this, but we were aware of the destruction and pain people overseas were experiencing.

The sense of doom, of a heavy black cloud covering what was beautiful and natural, was present, especially at bedtime. My bedroom was not a comfort. It was cold – we had no central heating and there were no rugs on the floors. The metal bed had squeaky bedsprings, a thin mattress and the only blanket was from the first world war – an army issue woollen blanket, slate coloured with a grey stripe. Armies must have used these in the time of the Boer War and perhaps they are still in use in Afghanistan today. I did not feel brave and for diversion I would imagine that the little holes in the green window blind were star constellations to which I gave names.

*

At the time of my divorce I had a dream that had some similarities with the recurring dreams of my pubescence. This dream was also very intense – it is still vivid and real today, thirty-four years later.

The Dream:

I am going up a stairway and I am looking into a grey cube of a room. In its centre is a brass bed, its head a curved delicate gold. Seated in the middle of this are three large dolls – girl-woman dolls. They sit back to back, each pointing to a different direction. Their dolls' articulated limbs do not move. Over each head is a cloth sack, tied at the throat by a thick cord. I am transfixed by these hooded heads for although the covering seems to be of a heavy cloth, through this tissue can be seen huge black cavities where eyes should be, cavities similar to the black eye cavities in skulls. I have read since that they are archetypal eyes of death – profound, implacable, like the eyes in the skulls around the house of the Russian goddess-witch Baba Yaga. They see beyond illusions and defences. They see not what might be good or bad but an unmasked reality.

The bedspread is black with a design of red cherries, yellow and white daisies and green leaves. Their colour is so intense that it vibrates. It is part of me. I resonate and not only do I see and feel but I hear sound – something harmonious, penetrating, beautiful.

For several years after this I try to capture that experience. I make a small painting in oil pastels. I try to do drawings of it, paintings, sculptures. But each effort seems so weak compared to the actual event that I am discouraged. Nevertheless, I continue to try.

Triform

The image of a doll woman, her head covered by a sack, her eye cavities black, persists in my work.

She stops appearing after I make three small girl-dolls with sacks over their heads and rope around their necks, and hang them from a tree.

Three Dolls

During this time, in sessions with Raymond, I am able to revisit my childhood. I am able to recall a time of innocence and a time of lost innocence. The first incident that clearly made me aware that we were different took place in the spring of 1938. I had just turned six. My father was sitting in his big rocking chair and I was sitting on his lap.

Childhood Memories: Starting School

This chair was no ordinary piece of furniture. It held a place of importance in our large living-and-dining-room. It sat apart from the rest of the furniture and was the focus for entertainment until the arrival of a new gleaming, streamlined floor model radio three years later. For now, it was a warm presence that recalled pleasant moments and promised the possibility of many more. Its black leather covering was held in place by bright brass tacks that were shaped like miniature volcanoes and that tasted cold and sour on my tongue. It had large flat wooden arms, unvarnished and discoloured where generations of hands had rested or pounded. It was easy to imagine that from this chair, gossip had been shared, problems had been solved, private moments of anguish had been rocked away, stories passed on and many songs sung.

My father continued the tradition and told us tales of "Ti-Jean" and "des Loups garou." He recited Victor Hugo's "La Chanson de Roland" and sang what he called a pot-pourri of French songs - some of which I would eventually teach to young school children.

This chair was wide enough for my brother and I to sit back to back. With feet firmly planted on the rockers and hands gripping the wide arms, we rocked happily back and forth singing with gusto "Jésus mon fort et mon rocher" (our favourite hymn taught us by Grandmère Brunet), or the songs so much loved by our father. Our mother, to my knowledge, never sat in that chair. But then, Mother did not sing - not ever.

Now that I was six I was telling my father how eager I was to go to school in the fall. Eager because I would be going with my best friend Georgette. She already was prepared and had her long-sleeved black dress with its pleated skirt, her white celluloid collar and cuffs, her long black stocking and her black shoes. Georgette was my very best friend – in fact, my only friend. When I had trouble getting to sleep, my mother would tell me to think of good things. My thoughts would be of rosy apples, pale green and pink, and of Georgette. She lived two doors away over her grandfather's general store, where we sampled the candies – little wax bottles filled with sweet red liquid and my favourite – flat pink and white marshmallow circles with a little chocolate man in the centre. Georgette's mother Bertha Boucher and my mother were close friends. They had little in common with their neighbours who had numerous children, who were devout, practicing Roman Catholics and who were part of large family living nearby. There was little or no communication with them.

    When I told my father that not only was I looking forward to going to school with Georgette but I was eager to have my black dress and stockings, he said, in his big stern voice (the voice of thunder, the voice that meant that it was useless to protest), "No, you are not going to L'école La Joie, you are going to a different school." I was numb with shock, struck dumb by this unbelievable news - unbelievable because Georgette and I were inseparable.

I do not recall any further talk about school that spring. My parents never referred to it and since I did not want to open a forbidden, dangerous topic, neither did I. During the two summer months, when as usual I was sent to the Eastern townships to my aunt Amabelle, her three daughters, older than I, patiently, but with much laughter taught me to say in English, *Yes, No,* and *May I have a glass of water please.* Thus I was prepared to enter Grade one at the Joliette Intermediate School in September, 1938.

Grade One: Joliette Intermediate School (Protestant) September, 1938

I don't remember how or with whom I got to school that first day. What I do remember is sitting at a desk, barely conscious of my surroundings. I did not dare to turn around or to look to my left where I knew there were rows of desks, inhabited by a large mass, and beyond this - the unknown. The desks were of highly varnished wood, resting on ornate wrought iron supports and bolted, not to the floor but to long narrow lengths of wood. This arrangement made it possible to move 5 desks, a row, at a time, to prepare for concerts, rummage sales or games.

My own desk had layers of varnish which gave it a look of taffy - the "tire" that my mother made every November 25th on "la fête de la Ste Catherine," la sainte des vieilles filles. I focused on this desk top for most of the day, and after the initial time of semi-consciousness, I began to examine the many markings carved in its surface. These were strange and interesting. Who had made them? When? Most importantly, what did they mean?

They were tangible evidence that I was not alone in my suffering, that others had been here in this very place. I was suffering, but in silence. With a shake of my head my long ringlets would fall on either side of my face making me feel protected. Not being able to see others I fancied that I could not be seen. It was a comfort to not see others seeing me. I could not understand what was happening around me. There was movement and sound, I was immersed in it but remained untouched - nothing penetrated. I felt vulnerable and unprotected and sensed danger. I wished that I had a box around me, a box like a telephone booth, with a window in the front and buttons to push to prevent sound from coming in. This would shield me from the meaningless noise of words that filled the air around me.

I was wearing a new dress, made by my mother for this occasion. It was of pale pink cotton organdy with an overall pattern of roses and pale green leaves, trimmed with emerald green rick-rack. It was a sundress, square-necked and sleeveless but with a little matching bolero, a style common in the thirties. Around my neck, on a very long chain, hung a large gold-coloured locket, not appropriate for school but since it was a gift from my father I had wanted to wear it. It would touch the desk when I leant forward and made a concrete connection between what was real and now, that is, Father, home, French, and what was new and frightening in this moment. And by far the most fearsome aspect of this day was the presence of our teacher, Mrs. Copping. She wanted to leave no doubt that she was in charge, and so from her chair behind the solid desk on a platform high above us she barked out her orders. When she stood she seemed so very tall to me. Her height was emphasized by the long vertical row of buttons, bells, that began at her high neckline and ended inches from the floor at her hem. Her hands fascinated me - they were like wax, the skin transparent over her very long, thin fingers. She would insert her little finger in one ear and move it very quickly up and down, a sight that never failed to amaze me. Four years later, after my brother had begun school, he, the engineer-to-be, took apart an alarm clock exposing its bell and its metal arms. When we saw the rapid motion of the arm against the bell we both exclaimed with surprised recognition: "Madame Copping!"

On this first day I did not take in my surroundings, nor could I distinguish students - they were part of a mass of moving, squirming entities. At some point in this very long first day I heard my name spoken in a clear, penetrating shrill "Elaine!" When I looked up, I heard "Stand up!" and understood that this meant for me to do as the others were doing. Then when others sat, I sat. It became a game, to be alert and to do what the others were doing. So the day passed - standing, sitting, sitting, sitting, and standing. A bell was rung. It was a hand bell rung by a designated student from the upper grades. School was over, and I was the last to leave.

Les Pierres de Paris

The necklace was kept in a special box in my parents' bedroom. The room had double doors that were paneled in rose-coloured glass, glass that was smooth on one side but patterned with ridges on the other. The ridges radiated from centres so that the panels seemed to be covered with stars. When my parents were at home, I was not allowed into this room. When they were away, it was understood that I might go in. I never entered the room immediately, but savoured the moment by pressing my face against the glass and looking into a room filled with slivers of pink light where familiar objects were transformed into mysterious shapes.

The special box that held the necklace was in the left-hand drawer of Mother's small vanity table. The table had an oval mirror and a recessed middle section flanked by two vertical drawers. Mother, who did not wear make-up, never used it for its intended purpose. When she brushed her long auburn hair, she never looked into the mirror but would coil it into a bun and pierce it fiercely with a hairpin that she had grimly held in her mouth. She always did things quickly, as if the present moment was not as important as what was to be done next.

The vanity table was used to hold the things that were precious and sacred to her. The ritual of touching these objects was done slowly and because they were always kept in the same places I could anticipate with pleasure the discovery of the familiar. Her Bible, which she kept nearest the bed, I usually opened first, for I liked the feel of the thin, delicate pages, edged in red gold, and wondered at their transparent strength. I would study the sixteen coloured illustrations, always saving my favourite for the last, an Arab beside the river Jordan. The scenery was pale and flat, but the colour of his long garment, a deep mauve, always made me catch my breath.

Other objects she kept in boxes in the vertical drawers. They were not just ornaments I was touching but links to stories of my mother's family, of events that happened long ago and in distant places. From a small blue box I would take out the delicate gold and tourquoise pendant, imagining my mother's oncle (uncle) Frédérick stumbling through the rubble of the San Francisco earthquake, picking up this trinket and years later giving it to my mother, a small girl. I was particularly fond of holding a small booklet that was covered with diamond-shaped pieces of mother-of-pearl that radiated soft hues of the rainbow. It had linen pages that kept sewing needles used many years ago by my great grandmother. The inscription in the central diamond-shaped piece, done in an elegant, very fine script, spelt 'Souvenir de Bertha.'

I always saved the box with the necklace of blue stones until last. It was of honey-coloured wood, long and narrow, with an unusual lid that, when opened, stayed attached to the box by two curious iron mechanisms, permitting the lid to stay behind the box and thus allowing a full view of the contents. The necklace belonged to La belle Bertha de Berne, my Swiss great grandmother. Before her marriage she had had a personal maid to do her hair but after coming to Namur, Quebec with her pastor husband, she had led a very different life - not one that she was used to. A relative of hers returning from Paris had brought her a necklace of blue stones, known in our family as 'Les pierres de Paris.' The stones were spheres, the colour of summer twilight, a soft blue that held shades of green. No two spheres were exactly alike. Looking into their smoky depths I would see magical worlds of intimate immensity.

A difficult landlord caused my father to decide to move. Our new place was on la rue Notre Dame. There, with no pink glass doors to create a world of magic, I made no more visits to Mother's vanity table. It seemed that I was shut out of her world of objects with their stories. But then one day she created a bridge to her world by offering me 'Les pierres de Paris,' saying I was now old enough to wear them. Wearing the necklace gave me a feeling of pride and excitement, for I felt that what I was entering into now was new territory.

On the way to school that first morning of wearing the necklace, I was followed by a boy on a bicycle. This boy had been following me for several days, riding very slowly, sometimes stopping, sometimes coming near and trying to get my attention by talking. I knew that he went to the

Roman Catholic school, l'école St. Viateur, and not the Protestant school I attended, Joliette Intermediate School. When he tried talking to me, I pretended to be indifferent. I felt vulnerable and afraid that he would turn out to be someone who would mock me and call me 'une maudite protestante' - words I had heard often enough that I dreaded them. In my anxiety I clutched at the necklace, and it broke - its blue stones scattering on grass and pavement. I was rigid with shock, but the boy quickly left his bicycle, knelt on his hands and knees and began picking up the stones. I was crying, making it difficult for me to find any of the stones. The boy found them all, even the small ones, and placed them in my hand. We did not talk or look at each other but I felt his nearness. When he placed the stones in my hand, a small pleasant shock of warmth spread from his hand to mine. I was not conscious of the time it took us to gather the stones, but we collected all of 'Les pierres de Paris.'

That afternoon when I came home from school with the broken necklace I wanted so much to speak to my mother about my feelings. I had glimpsed a new world, one that was still strange to me, but that I was closer to knowing.

Les Pierres de Paris

Kettle Drums

The New Brunswick symphony is playing at a concert at the Capitol Theatre in Moncton. Much to my delight there is a percussion section. I look at the kettledrums and I am transported to another time.

It is Montréal, la rue Jeanne Mance, the month is June and the year 1936 - I am four years old. Mother and I are visiting mon oncle Emile. This is a dutiful visit, done once a year and always in the summer.

Emile Flümann is Mother's uncle - her mother's brother. Tante Delima, his wife is Mother's father's sister. So this visit fulfills a double duty.

I am grateful to be sitting on the smooth blue brocade sofa - not on the despicable plush one, which, because of the heat and my bare legs can be almost unbearable.

Mon oncle sits in his big chair facing my mother and me. He is the focus of the room - an impressive presence, immobile, mute but dominating nevertheless. Beside him on a small table there is the usual delicate long-stemmed white clay pipe. We speak to him but he rarely answers. When he smiles, there is something awkward about his face and the crinkles move around one eye only. I am curious about the metal strap over one shoe under his trouser leg. In spite of the heat he is always dressed in a wool suit - cuffed trousers, vest, and jacket. There are others in the room but their words have nothing to do with me. I am in my silent world and do not connect with the conversations flowing over me, like warm water.

The door to Cousine May's room is half open, and inside I can see the two large kettle drums. The sight of the glimmering warm copper of these is the delight, the high point of my visit. I lose myself in their golden, fiery glow. It is the only tenderness I feel in the room. My mother who is near me does not radiate tender feelings. I am aware of her fear, which prevents her from being free to express herself. She is afraid of being humiliated, of being judged. She does not have the confidence to be herself. Perhaps she does not yet know her own truth.

A tight silence, oppressive, encloses her. I

absorb this but can do nothing. I sense that I would be betraying her if I did not imitate her. What I do is lose myself in the gleaming welcoming warmth of the copper. I'm aware of the presence of the clay pipe - so comforting to see it there on each visit. Finally, my gaze comes slowly round to the clock under glass on the mantle. I am certain that it will never stop its smooth silent comforting motion. Here is something to be relied upon, something that can be trusted, that is free, that is self sufficient, that does not need comforting. It is something complete in itself - nothing is secret or hidden, no emotion. It just moves smoothly back and forth, back and forth.

My Brother Edward Thomas

Mother made sure that we knew his name was Edward – pronounced à la English and not the French 'Edouard'. Her mother, a Swiss protestant whose main language was French, nevertheless did not want to be associated with French Canadians who were 99% Roman Catholic and considered by her family to be an inferior race. Mother lived this prejudice which must have caused her difficulties because my father, although Protestant, was a 'pure laine' Québecois. Grandmother tolerated him because of his religion but she never let an opportunity pass without correcting his French. With a bland expression seen only in her presence he would refer to 'Holiette' (Joliette), 'deuce' (deux), 'pétraves' (betteraves) and would ask her to 'dégreyez-vous' (literally, unrig yourself). She never failed to react immediately and showed no interest in the origins of these Québecois expressions.

At home, Edward was called 'Gars-Gars' (pronounced Gaw-Gaw) or 'Ti-Gars' or, only by my mother, 'Mon beau 'ptit bébé bleu' crooned in a voice trembling with emotion. I was 'la 'ptite' or, for some reason known only to my mother, 'la drine'. This title always made me feel ashamed and humiliated, for if there was warmth in the tone used to refer to me as 'la drine' I did not feel it. It made me feel apart, different, not quite human. I was able to keep it secret at school until one fateful day in Grade six, when all 32 children of our school were pounding up the stairs at recess, shouting "La drine, la drine". My mischievous little brother was responsible. After this 'La drine' was never mentioned again. It was no longer a family secret. I had been humiliated enough. Episode closed.

My first glimpse of Edward was early in the morning of February 22nd, 1936. He had just been born. As was the custom then, babies were born at home and siblings were sent to a neighbour's during the birthing. I do not remember where I had spent the night but I do recall vividly being brought in to my parents' bedroom early that dark morning. This was a place where I was never permitted to enter. My mother was in bed. I had never seen her in bed. Her long auburn hair was not in its usual bun but was free, covering her shoulders with its shimmering copper and gold. It looked so alive that I wanted to touch it.

Beside her was something new – a bundle of sky blue cloth. I was told that this was 'mon 'ptit frère'. There had been no mention of his expected arrival, no preparation. Being only three years and ten months old I accepted without surprise whatever the adults presented ... so ... I had a little brother.

The most wonderful thing about this event for me was not the arrival of a new baby but the fact that this baby was complete. When Mother drew back the soft blue wrap she exposed his tiny hands and I was transfixed – he had delicate, pink, perfect miniature fingernails. A marvel.

Later that day my best friend Georgette, who lived two doors down the street from us, was also presented with a baby brother, Bernard. Bernard was skinny and pale, with dry, scaly skin, whereas Edward, who weighed ten pounds, had pink skin, blue eyes, and blond hair. Such colouration was rare in French Canada and therefore considered special. We accepted Edward but did not talk about Bernard.

Georgette and I were told by my father that it was Indians who had brought us the babies. I imagined an Indian wearing a huge feathered headdress like the one on the cover of one of my storybooks. He would be carrying a large brown sack over his shoulder, as did Santa Claus or le Bonhomme Sept Heures. (Bonhomme Sept Heures put any child who was not in bed by seven o'clock into his sack.) I thought that the Indian must have been kept very busy bringing babies to houses and collecting children. Where he brought them from was a mystery. There were many new babies on our street but I never noticed if any children disappeared. I didn't want to know.

My early memories of 'mon frère' are many and varied, in the same way that his adventures were many and varied. He had a large head (we French Canadians called these 'des têtes carrées' (square heads), fine blondish hair, a lisp (he couldn't say words with 'r' until he began school), and eyes that my mother said were like the sea, at times a grey-green, other times smoky-blue. When he was excited they became black.

They were black the day he came running breathless into the kitchen, his singed eyebrows giving his face a new look, imploring Mother "Dis-le pas à Papa" (Don't tell Papa). He'd taken Father's corn pipe, and he and Marcel, his friend from next door, had tried to smoke shredded Montreal Herald paper.

They were black when he was gripped by his obsession for plugging openings with whatever was at hand – nails, screws, blocks of wood. Mother had a hard time removing a swollen wood block he'd stuck in the drain hole of her new wringer washing machine. She was never able to remove a large screw stuck in the silver fuel holder of a silver heirloom egg cooker. It is still there.

I admired his courage. He liked to try new things. For example, one day when he was three he had been unusually quiet. Mother should have checked up on him but she hadn't. He had taken Father's drill brace and bit, a tool almost as tall as himself, and had successfully drilled a hole in the front room floor. This was a room that was used only when my parents sang and played the large table piano. When Mother saw the hole her lips became a tight line – something we grew to dread. She said the classic "attend que ton père arrive" (wait until your father gets here). When Father entered the house and saw, in the room next to the hall, Mother, me, and the culprit around the hole in the floor, his colour changed to bright red. I thought that he would roar – he had a very big voice, like thunder, frightening.

Before he could do this, my brother, who had been balancing from one foot to the other, arms behind his back (a pose copied from Father), said, in a calm, serious voice, the voice of one adult speaking to another, "*Ça prend un Christ de fou pour faire ça, eh Papa?*" ("It takes one hell of a fool to do such a thing, eh Father?")

In my family it is my brother who is noticed. He is blond, blue-eyed, charming, courageous, and very intelligent. I am the obverse – silent, admiring, invisible. I am alone, separate, lost, without identity. The Savignac incident has left me with a terrible legacy, exacerbated because I have no one to talk to. I have no voice.

Gate 6

At the entry to Gate Six
I am stripped of a piece of my regalia:
My complacency

The cancer has left me. I have found my way out of the woods – one step at a time. Raymond has helped me to see that the cancer was my friend. Without it I would not have had the opportunity to understand my past and to emerge from this past ready for a new life. I thank the cancer and I let it go.

Then one day I come upon a sentence from a text by St. Cyril that impresses me: "While on the road beware of the dragon by the wayside." The words stay with me and I realize that this is another "coincidence" that I must pay attention to. Something overwhelming is about to happen along this new road. To prepare for this event I must return to Raymond.

With several deep breaths I enter another session, eyes closed. I descend into an underworld. When my feet touch bottom I am on a smooth road.

I see a horse. I mount it and we continue along the road. From the tangle by the road I see the flames issuing from the dragon's mouth.

Femme à la rencontre d'un dragon

Then the dragon emerges, large, fierce.

Dragon Breathing Fire

I am terrified and so is my horse. Raymond asks me to dismount and to touch the dragon. Because I trust Raymond I reach out and touch the flank of the dragon. The beast immediately stops his fire-breathing and without words between us I know that he is now my friend.

Raymond suggests that I ask the dragon to help me. The creature dives into a deep dark lake that suddenly appears beside the road. He brings up a jewel – a large star sapphire, which he gives to me. We both gaze at it. It is very beautiful, giving off a bright blue light.

Dragon with Sapphire

I am living or discovering what the German poet Rilke said: "Perhaps all the dragons in our lives are princesses who are only waiting to see us act, just once, with beauty and courage. Perhaps everything that frightens us is in its deeper essence something helpless that needs our love."

Woman with Dragon

With Raymond's help I'm able to return to the past.

I am back in time – fifteen years old.

I am in Quebec City – in Saint John's Hall.

It is night, but I cannot sleep.

I tremble. My teeth chatter.

I cannot put words to my feelings.

The sounds of the city, the lights, the people – everything has become so strange.

There are thirty other students here. The persons in charge are a United Church minister and his wife. They are remote, inaccessible. Bells rule our lives – for getting up, for meals, for study hour, for lights out.

We eat in the basement, a dark place that never sees the sun. There are two cooks. Seen in this shadowy place they could be characters from a Grimm's fairy tale. They are D.P.s (Displaced Persons) who, we learn later, have fled disaster in Europe to find a place here with us. We eventually become fond of them. Mrs. Ralston has an enormous goiter. Her frail husband has a peculiar head – a straight line could be drawn from the back of his head to his buttocks. They do not look well, and in fact they will eventually be found to be tubercular, but not before several students are infected.

My roommate is Jeanny. We've been friends for five years. She stayed with us during the winter months of school. With her, I feel secure. Together we explore this old city, holding hands. Her older brother Mike, who is also at the Hall, suggests gently that to walk hand in hand together is considered peculiar. He also advises me that to play Mozart or hymns on the common room piano is inappropriate.

At Thanksgiving I go home, to many changes.

We no longer live in the city, but in Base-de-Roc, in Tante Lily's house. Tante Lily is my mother's aunt, who is very ill (she dies the following year). Her son, 'mon oncle' Eugène, asks my mother to look after Tante and to care for Raymond, her challenged 45-year-old son who is unable to look after himself.

In Base-de-Roc I have no bedroom and, of course, no furniture. There is no room for our piano, so it was given to a friend. It was a large heavy black table model, with only 84 keys, and with heavy carved legs. On it I could pound out my frustrations, my anger but also my joy. I will miss it.

My cat Tiger-Lily is no longer with us. Mother simply says that Tiger-Lily is gone. I do not ask when. Tiger-Lily had been with us for ten years – a big, lovable cat with double paws, white with a cap of gold stripes. I had taught him to drink milk using a doll's baby bottle. He would allow himself to be dressed in a bonnet, and would lie down, covered by a baby blanket, in my doll's carriage, his front paws around the bottle, his back paws supporting it.

Our furniture is stored in a shed Father has built in the back of the house. My brother, who is a cowboy at this time and wears boots, hat, and shirt like those of Roy Rogers, calls this shed a saloon. He has a roulette wheel that is rigged so that it always stops at the same number. He also makes a huge hangman's noose and wants to call the place The Hangman's Saloon, but my father gently persuades him to take it down. Our next door neighbour's son had been found guilty of murdering the school's janitor and was subsequently hung. Adults never talked of this in front of children so we concluded that the crime was not simply one of murder. Homosexuality was involved – a silent subject at this time.

It is good to be home with my parents, and especially to be with my young brother who has so much to tell me that he follows me into the bathroom, sitting on a large wicker laundry basket while he continues talking. I love him. But I feel very deeply the losses of bedroom furniture, my own bedroom, my cat, and my piano, and I have no way as yet to mourn.

Eclipse

His name was Alberto. When I first pronounce it, placing the accent on the last syllable, as we do in French, he corrected me. "C'est Al̲berto!" He was Italian.

The war had been over for two years, and he and his sister Maria had just arrived from Italy to be with their Grandmother Nicoletti. They did not talk of the war. Life on the farm in Base-de-Roc, a farm only a little farther down the road from Tante Lily's where my family lived at the time, must have been a very different experience.

It was summer. I was on holiday from boarding school, glad to be home. Base-de-Roc was new to me. I knew none of our neighbours, but an opportunity to know them came when our barn cat had four kittens. We already had three cats so homes had to be found for the kitts. I bicycled down 'le rang Base-de-Roc,' met and chatted with the farmers' wives, found homes for the cats and was delighted to meet Maria and Alberto.

He was foreign looking, exotic, with full lips, grey eyes and skin the colour of olives. Olives that I had first tasted recently in Tante Alice's kitchen. Olives that were, to me, unusually strange, so smooth with their out-of-the-ordinary taste, mysterious with their stuffing of something a surprising red.

I remember him as always being astride his bicycle. When he stopped to talk he would take a cigarette out of a pack that he kept in his shirt pocket, insert it in an ivory-coloured holder, hold this against his chest, and, to emphasize a point, would gesture with it elegantly. I thought this a striking pose, fascinating, as I did his accent, so different from that of the local boys.

My young brother was not impressed with Alberto. He considered him affected – a fake, a fraud. Words were not strong enough to show his contempt; therefore, when Alberto rode by on his bicycle, my brother would make loud, extravagant, exaggerated retching noises.

That year, during the Thanksgiving holiday, Alberto and I occasionally bicycled together. One evening we found ourselves on an unknown road – deserted, no cars, no houses, no nearby trees. It was quiet, no bird song, only the large, huge sky. It was my favourite time of day – 'entre chien et loup.' The sun had set but the night had not yet come. The sky was a transparent glass-like blue green. It was a magical moment, a feeling of being suspended in time. The sun had left us, the unknown was about to present itself.

We stopped and were still astride our bicycles. Without a word we looked at a huge full October moon. As we looked, a red shadow appeared in it, and as we gazed, spellbound, the moon became a deep red. We turned toward each other and very softly, tentatively, tenderly, our lips touched. We were filled with awe, lost for words and not wanting to break this spell of wonderment. We silently left that moment of enchantment.

Gate 7

At the entry to Gate Seven
I am stripped of a piece of my regalia:
My sanity

I am in remission. I am waiting for the dragon to make his re-appearance. Sacks continue to appear in my work, sometimes as fruit fallen from trees, sometimes as growths around underground roots, sometimes as soft cloth sculptures, always white – symbols of abundance. Their openings are tied with rope so their contents are unknown. They are never opened.

Then an incident brings everything to a head. While driving with a friend on St. George Street in Moncton, I glimpse a man holding the hand of a very pregnant woman. In his other hand he holds a large, full, green plastic garbage bag. I see them only for an instant before they vanish from sight, disappearing between buildings at the corner of St. George and Highfield Street.

This image keeps recurring, unbidden, and with such force that I can feel the impact physically, in my gut. I am no longer in control of my thoughts. I feel I am a powerful engine, going at full speed, that has lost its governor. I cannot stop nor slow down. This condition bewilders me and frightens me enough to make me seek the help of a psychiatrist friend.

At the end of our first session the psychiatrist asks me to draw what was in the garbage bag – the sack. The idea stuns me, for I have never dared to open up the sacks that appear in my works and in my dreams. But since this one isn't mine (or so I think at the time), I am able to take courage and look. Twenty charcoal drawings are the result.

The first is the most powerful. This sack contains several skulls, the eye cavities black, profound, implacable; three large, red, erect penises; a small green snake; and, at the bottom, a little plant sprouting one new green leaf.

Sac noir

All the other drawings are portraits of a dark-haired man, naked, his eyes obscured by a black line. Sometimes he is in the coils of a very large python.

Empoisonné

Other times he is only a head, filling the sack. Always his expression is one of Christ-like anguish.

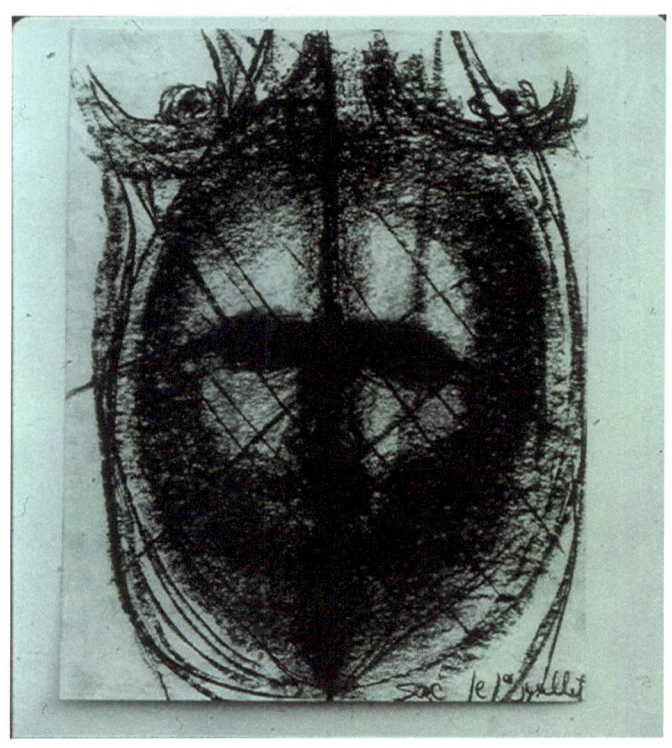

Sac 1992

Dans le sac, tête

The last drawing – the image that stops me from drawing more – is of a man standing with his arms folded across his chest. He is a life-like portrait of my father, and because this is not done consciously, it makes me gasp.

Memory, 1992

I bring this drawing to Father Bujold who says with satisfaction, *"On peut commencer maintenant."* ("Now we can begin.")

*

In the words of Beaudelaire: *"Once we have burned our brains out, we can plunge to Hell or Heaven – any abyss will do – deep in the unknown to find the new."*

*

I have been seeing Raymond Bujold for two years. With imagery, I have experienced many adventures. Almost always I have put these images on paper afterwards – usually making paper collages of the scenes that presented themselves, and usually without words. I have gone through a year of grieving, a year of upheaval. I am newly retired from my teaching profession, a profession that was part of my identity. My pension is very small since I spent twenty years as a housewife and only a little over a decade as a teacher. I have severed a fifteen-year, off-and-on poisonous relationship with a man. (It was really more an association than a relationship.) I feel vulnerable. I no longer have the cloak of financial security nor a professional garment. Alone, I phone friends to talk about wildflowers, or to ask if the bed in their spare room is available. I need to be with other people, need to feel that security. I, who was always so quiet, agreeable, and cooperative, have become aggressive, use foul language, grow impatient easily, shout my complaints. But at least I have the sense to ask for help – from friends who are part of a self-help group which listens to my rantings and gives no advice or comments but is there if I need someone to talk with at 2 am.

I had expected some upheaval, but when it happened I am almost overwhelmed by its strength. I see Raymond weekly but have little memory of what happens in these sessions. I ask the psychiatrist friend if I have just experienced a psychosis. She says, "No, you have been grieving."

The Grieving: My Uncle, Charles

I grieve for Charles, the uncle who lived with us, who was more a brother than an uncle, who went to war, never to return. When he was with us, there seemed to be more warmth and energy, a lightness and gaiety, more vitality in our home.

He was not a tall man, but was muscular, quick, powerful – a boxer in his leisure time. I remember his sea-green eyes, his cropped curly red hair, his freckles, his mischievous smile. Since then I've found men with these features very attractive, and I realize that my first husband possessed many of them. My Grandmother often commented with pleasure on this fact.

Charles's departure for overseas was very quiet. He seemed to know he would never come back. This attitude was in sharp contrast to that of his older brother, Arthur, who was eager to go. Arthur became a fighter pilot and returned a war hero. He was given the keys to Montreal.

Before he left, Charles gave Mother a special gift, a pin in the form of silver wings with the insignia of the RCAF. He was very close to my mother, who had left school at the age of 15 to look after her ill mother, her baby brothers Arthur and Charles and Charles's twin, Charlotte (Lise).

His dog Scottie, a rat-terrier, small, custard-coloured and very lively, stayed with us. Charles told my brother and me to look after his bicycle, his skis, and his bed with its sturdy maple board. He left behind a trunk containing photos, letters, objects, mementos of his short life. On her yearly visit, my grandmother would take out these objects, return them lovingly to the trunk, and weep.

I don't remember exactly when we received a telegram from the war office telling us Charles was missing in action. It seemed a long time later that we were told he had died on October 20, 1943. He had been rear gunner in a Lancaster bomber that was downed over Hamburg.

We never had a gathering to talk of him, to grieve. There was no funeral. No one sent their condolences. We had a heavy dull feeling of emotions held back.

I don't remember what happened to Scottie. The loss of the little dog makes me remember Charles's absence, and I weep.

The Grieving: My Husband, Andy

Alexander Taylor Anderson. Your family call you Alec, but you ask friends to call you Andy. For at least four generations the first son of the Andersons is name Alexander. You dissociate from that tradition, choosing to omit the Alexander as the name for your own first-born son. It can't be that you dislike the Scots heritage, for you call your daughter Heather and your second son Robert Bruce. The latter is named after your mother's father, a stern Presbyterian minister – a powerful man who helped form the Untied Church of Canada, who became Principal of Queen's University, but who disowned his favourite daughter when she divorced. You inherit his love of sailing but not his sternness. You are tender, compassionate, with a love of people and animals and plants.

I have a vivid memory of you – my first view of you.

It is summer.

We are in Base-de-Roc.

You have just brought my parents back from Quebec City where you were best man at your partner / best friend's wedding. The bride is a cousin of my mother's, one of Tante Lily's granddaughters.

You are leaning on your new car. It is a metallic blue colour that glitters in the bright sun. You are at ease, wearing a blue suit, one that repeats the blue of the car – a soft blue, like that of the sky in springtime. You wear the suit well. You are at ease, comfortable in your body.

Andy – A Dream

You are smiling, a large smile that lights up your face. You seem to glow – to have sunshine within you. Your hair is so fair it is almost white, a fine pure gold.

But what I find most extraordinary is your gaze. You have blue eyes – eyes that are open, not veiled, eyes that invite but are not intrusive. They are of such an intense, cobalt blue that they seem to cast a blue light.

You and your partner, John, have a turkey farm. Ten thousand birds that are free range.

You have a good name and good customers. What pleasure you must feel when Wilder Penfield's wife always requests your largest bird, insisting that the feet be left on.

Then there are the unusual incidents that you must remember.

There is the time you and John make an unexpected and grand entrance at one of the posh restaurants in downtown Montreal. You are delivering five turkeys, large, dead, and plucked, with head and feet left on. The elevator malfunctions, and you are left stuck between floors. The only solution is to crawl out of it after having flung the five dead birds ahead of you. You find yourselves on the gleaming floor, in the softly lit atmosphere of the elegant restaurant. Like true Montrealers none of the diners pays any attention to the five bodies and to the two men in coveralls crawling on hands and knees out of an opening near the floor. That is, they pretend not to pay any attention.

There is the time you make a delivery to a residence high on the mountain in Westmount, to the home of a former school friend. She is having a party, and you are bringing a turkey. It is raining, so a footman with an umbrella escorts you to the door. You are in overalls and holding a large dead turkey – not a pretty sight. Yet you remain your usual self – at ease, good-humoured.

But isn't the best entertainment giving speeches to the ten thousand birds on the range? We shout long, impassioned speeches ending with an even louder shout of 'Down with Duplessis!' (Duplessis being a premier of Quebec, known for corruption.) After a pause the turkeys show their approval by raising their ugly, skinny necks and in unison respond with 'Golu Golu' or, in English,

'Gobble Gobble.' We experience the heady sense of power politicians must feel as they illicit applause from a crowd. After this I can no longer attend any political rally without the vision of thousands of turkeys, mindlessly but obediently reacting en masse to a volley of words.

While you and John farm, I finish my first year of teaching, then accept a scholarship to a university in Alabama, as part of an international house program. The French-speaking students that I meet here – from France, Belgium and Switzerland – become life-long friends. The daily letters you send help me overcome my 'mal du pays.' When you write asking me to marry you, in April, I cancel my plans to visit Mexico and tour the western United States with Francine, my Belgian friend, and I go home in May. We decide to wait one year before marriage, for I need a year of teaching to make my certificate permanent and you hope that within that time your farm will prosper.

It does not.

It could have, for you and your partner are well prepared, holding Bachelor of Science degrees in agriculture from MacDonald College, McGill

University. You are young, strong, healthy, energetic. The customers your mother gave you are many, and they are from Westmount. But their business is not enough to offset a bad piece of luck. At Thanksgiving and again at Christmas, American producers begin dumping in our market. Furthermore, you are the victim of a large theft one silent, snowy night. You try to form a co-operative with local farmers, but the communication problems between you (English speaking) and the French speaking farmers make this plan unworkable.

It is a sad time. You have such a good name for the farm – the Merry Thought. Your mother says it is Scots for wishbone, so the M is made up of two interlocking wishbones. On the rear of the farm vehicle is the slogan, 'Let's Talk Turkey.'

You and I are married in June, after I finish my year of teaching. You and John realize that the Merry Thought cannot support two families. John and his wife stay on for a year, and you return to work for the company that hired you just after you graduated from McGill.

It is not a good move. You are unable to do what you most want to do – to farm. Instead, to earn a living for a wife and child you become a salesman, a situation that you find very stressful. You seek a solution to this situation in drink. I, in denying that there is a problem and in becoming more and more controlling, find my own solution. Our three children suffer. The tension in the home is unbearable. We are unable to help each other. We go to doctors for help and finally decide to lead separate lives.

Before we make a final separation we see a social worker – an intelligent man who listens to us, who listens in particular to our dreams. Mine – I am living under ice. The ice is very thick, clear like glass, with only small grooves in its upper surface.

It is thick ice, but it is warm.

Your dream – you are in a queue, a long line of people who are buying tickets to a ball game. You wait a long time but when your turn finally comes, the wicket closes.

This dream is repeated.

We are unable to continue with this social worker because a grant that supported him runs out. We are no longer able to get the help we so badly need. We cannot solve our problems.

In an unmasked moment you tell me that you know you drink too much, but to stop means you will have to look at yourself. You say that you do not want to do that, that you cannot do that.

Five years later, surrounded by village people who care for you, but who, one by one, after trying to help, have come to the realization that they are powerless to do anything without your decision to change – five years later you are alone.

Your mother, who lives in Montreal, is put in a special care home and can no longer communicate with you.

Your close neighbour's fifteen-year-old daughter cannot tolerate the thought of going to school by bus where she will be harassed because she is French Canadian, and she kills herself with a gun. It is early September. A few days later, on your fifty-fourth birthday, you do the same.

I remember the verse from the book of Esther:

When Mordecai perceived all that was done,
Mordecai rent his clothes, and put on sackcloth
With ashes, and he went out into the midst of the city
And cried with a loud and bitter cry.
- Esther, Chapter 4, Verse 1

I want to do the same, but I hold it in. Only much later, in 1992, the year of anguish and insanity, do I allow the grieving to take place.

The End of Grieving: Touching Bottom

Raymond Bujold helps me mourn these losses of so many years ago. He also guides me through my other losses – the lost 'relationship', my lost profession, my diminished income. I have touched bottom. I feel helpless – like the corpse Innana hung from a meat hook. The long slow fall has come to an end.

Ascent

During the Ascent my regalia is restored.

Blessed Illusion

Louisa, an artist friend, finds me one day and gives me a poem to read. It is called "Last Night," by Antonio Machado. The second stanza, as translated by Robert Bly, reads:

> *Last night, as I was sleeping,*
> *I dreamt – marvelous error! –*
> *That I had a beehive*
> *Here inside my heart.*
> *And the golden bees*
> *Were making white combs*
> *And sweet honey*
> *From my old failures.*

The father of a friend, a man who knows both Spanish and French, remarks that 'marvelous error' in the French translation is 'illusion bénit,' or 'blessed illusion' in English, and that the word 'failures' translates into the French word 'rancunes'

– in English, perhaps more accurately as grudges or resentments.

*

The idea of transforming resentments into something beautiful so moves me that I do several paintings showing a woman, golden bees and light. The woman stands in a golden glow, a red-gold heart/womb with bees emanating and surrounding her.

Bee Woman, with Honeycomb

Bee Woman, with Spiral

She is sometimes flanked by two cats.

Bee Woman, with Cats

I remember that the artist Yvon Gallant, in the year he painted large portraits (10' x 10'), did one of me that showed bees about my head. The theme of transformation, or renewal, is clear, for that painting was chosen for the lobby of the oncology department of our Georges Dumont Hospital.

Portrait of Elaine

Ally

I am often asked why moose appear so often in my art. Sometimes they appear with golden antlers, in a dark landscape dominated by a silver full moon.

Moose, under a Full Moon

At other times in a winter scene of white.

Elan d'esperance

But most often they appear in a dark forest, the sky filled with winged creatures, and, in the foreground, a young child touching the flank of this large, powerful beast.

Moose, with Child and Winged Creatures

Our Native people go on vision quests to return after a mystical encounter with the image of an animal that represents them – an animal that is their icon. The moose that appears in a last visualization session with Raymond is, for me, such an animal. In that session, I descend into my past and relive a time in my childhood when I am surrounded by greyness, by indifferent, cold people, people who humiliate me and do not protect or nourish. Suddenly, silently and without my bidding, there appears an immense moose. With his huge antlers he scoops up the grey people and hurls them far away. He does not hurt them, he just removes them from my presence.

Ally

Afterwards, I place my hands on his flank and feel his strength. His warmth and his goodness resonate in me. He is my protector, my ally. This experience is the most vivid of many encounters during my descents into the dark unconscious depths.

I let go of the past painful childhood experiences, and I come to realize that I have the strength and newfound life to begin the ascent.

Take Joy

Early one morning, while I am not quite awake, out of the darkness come the words: "YOU MUST BE SILENT." They come unbidden, in a voice that is felt rather than heard. With them comes calm.

I am able to welcome this stillness and it becomes a vital part of my ascent into a world that is so different from the dark one left behind.

*

I go to see the psychic, Shirley T. I've gone to her before, as have several of my artist friends. She helps us unlock doors, unblock creativity.

This time she is very positive. She says I am on the right path, and predicts that shortly I will meet and marry a man who is tall, fair, with blue eyes, that he and I have been on similar paths, that soon our paths will converge.

*

As usual with predictions, I store them but do not dwell on them, much less expect them. In my new peaceful stillness I have no interest in marrying again.

Then, I have a vivid dream, of bathing in a pool of dark but warm water. As I emerge from the pool, a tall man is standing there to put, protectively, a large towel around me. I do not see him, but I feel his presence, warmth, and a knowledge that I've always known this man, that we are fated to be together.

Some weeks later, on July 19th, I go to my favourite outdoor café where I sit at a table that is already occupied by a tall man. We talk, and he tells me he is here to open a bookstore of rare and second-hand books. I am delighted, for in my travels my first stop in a new town is to browse in a bookstore of second-hand books.

Friends see him with a dog the size of a horse. It is identified as an Akita.

I tell myself, he probably also has a young lover.

I go to Ottawa with family for three weeks and upon my return I enter the newly opened Attic Owl Bookstore. I return often, with friends or with a granddaughter. I like being near this bookseller. Beside him, I experience the same feeling that was present in my dream of the tall stranger wrapping me in the towel when I emerged from the pool, the stranger I felt I had always known. And although his eyes are more green than blue, he is tall and fair!

When we talk, we never seem to have time to finish our conversations. One day he says just this, and I quickly ask him to come to dinner at my house on Saturday.

He agrees.

I ask if he likes rosemary chicken. He says yes. I serve three different dishes of vegetables from my garden. We talk, and we talk. I forget to serve the chicken. He forgets to ask for it.

He helps with the cleaning up, and discovers the forgotten chicken. We laugh together. I give him some of the chicken to take to Halifax the following day, when he is going to see his daughter.

*

So begins a friendship, of long walks with the Akita, of visits with friends, trips to Halifax to see his daughter. But what I enjoy most are our conversations, the talks we never want to end. He reads me some of his poems. I translate one into French.

Our friendship soon changes. We fall in love, and decide to marry. We choose the anniversary of our meeting, July 19th of the following year, as our day of marriage.

Our wedding is a joyful celebration, bringing together a community of friends and of family. We begin a life together.

> *The gloom of the world*
> *Is but a shadow;*
> *Behind it,*
> *Yet within reach,*
> *Is Joy.*
> *Take Joy.*
>
>   - Fra Giovanni, 1513

Woman Present to Her Past

Acknowledgements

The Breach House Gang, nine Moncton-area writers, have supported me in many ways during the writing of this memoir. I would especially mention Elizabeth Blanchard, Lee D. Thompson, and Noeline Bridge. I also want to thank Jean Humphreys and Elizabeth Yeoman for their close reading of the manuscript and for their many helpful comments. Maggie Dominic encouraged me in the beginning and without her kind words and example I would never have got started. This book is dedicated to my husband, Ed Lemond, without whom it would not yet exist.

www.ingramcontent.com/pod-product-compliance
Lightning Source LLC
Chambersburg PA
CBHW041203230426
43673CB00035B/499